Good
spent together friendships, peace.
no hard feelings
Sacrificing 1 thing for principle
learned, organized
better
Greeks kept on in spite of everything
& had games.

spirit
ideals don't die
visionaries
revivals of ideals
cooperation
a clean project.

former transitory
ideals are lasting

10 Fred
O. stay

Mr. T.
Mill.

don't you
gather

what good would
it do?
Its broken now.

MAN AND THE MASSES

Setting by Lee Simonson *Photograph by Francis Bruguiere*

Scene III from The Theatre Guild Production

MAN AND THE MASSES

(MASSE MENSCH)

A Play of the Social Revolution
in Seven Scenes

BY
ERNST TOLLER

TRANSLATED BY
LOUIS UNTERMEYER

THE THEATRE GUILD VERSION,
WITH SIX ILLUSTRATIONS
FROM PHOTOGRAPHS OF THE
THEATRE GUILD PRODUCTION

GARDEN CITY NEW YORK
DOUBLEDAY, PAGE & COMPANY
1924

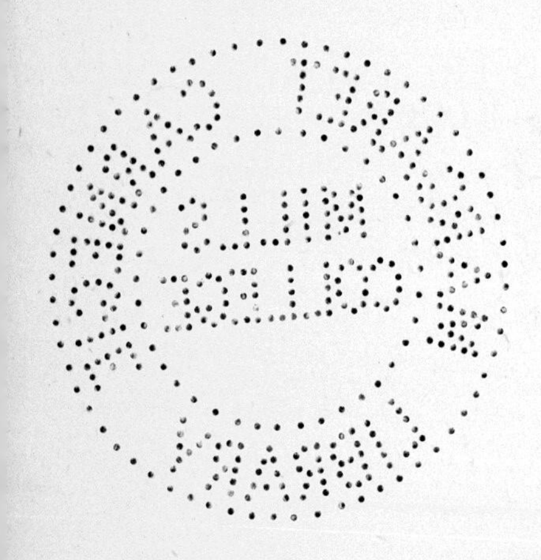

PRINTED IN THE UNITED STATES
AT
THE COUNTRY LIFE PRESS, GARDEN CITY, N. Y.

First Edition

World Revolution.
Bearer of New Forces.
Bearer of New Folk-Unity.
The Century is a red glare.
Pyres are bloody with guilt.
Earth crucifies itself.

DEDICATED TO
THE PROLETARIAT

(The first draft of this play was made in October, 1919, in the first year of the German Revolution. It was written in the military prison at Niederschönenfeld.)

CHARACTERS

WORKMEN

WORKWOMEN

THE NAMELESS ONE

OFFICER

PRIEST

MAN (An Official)

SONIA IRENE L. (The Woman)

FIGURES IN THE VISION

SONIA IRENE L. (The Woman)

THE COMPANION

BANKERS

THE OFFICIAL

SENTINELS

PRISONERS

SHADOWS

(The second, fourth, and sixth pictures are visionary; projections of a dream.)

FOREWORD TO THE GERMAN SECOND EDITION*

(*A Letter to a Creative Producer*)

There are critics who complain that, although the "dream scenes" are already sufficiently dream-like, you gave the "realistic scenes" a visionary air, and that thus you blur the boundary between dream and reality. I wish emphatically to declare that you have altogether realized my intention. These "realistic" pictures are no typical naturalistic scenes. With the exception of Sonia, the types are not individualized. What can be realistic in my drama "Man and the Masses"? Only the spiritual, the intellectual qualities. As a politician, I rate the individual, the group, the official, the protagonist, the economic factor, as actualities. As an artist, I question these "realistic" occurrences. ("It is still a question whether we personally exist.")

In a prison yard I see prisoners saw wood in monotonous rhythm. Men, I think feelingly. This one may be a labourer; that one, a peasant; yonder, perhaps, a court clerk. I see the room in which the labourer

* *This is a translation of the Foreword to the German Second Edition which appeared in 1922.—L. U.*

to the bourgeois seems "deep" and "important" as an expression of most agitating mental conflict, leaves the proletariat quite unmoved.

I need not emphasize that proletariat art, no less than all other, must spring from a human source, must in its depths be all-encompassing, all-enfolding, like life, like death. There is a proletariat art only in so far as its creator shapes the manifold forms of proletariat life and feeling into the eternal humanities.

ERNST TOLLER.

FORTRESS OF NIEDERSCHÖNENFELD,
October, 1921.

INTRODUCTION

I

"Man and the Masses," that agonized drama of a people's revolution and self-revelation, was written in a Bavarian prison by a man in his mid-twenties. Possibly no better background can be given to the work itself than the autobiography which Toller has furnished for an introductory study of his plays ("Ernst Toller und seine Bühnenwerke") written by Fritz Droop. Toller writes thus about himself:

> Born December 1, 1893, at Samotschin, County Bromberg.* His father, Max Toller, a merchant, died when the boy was sixteen. At first he attended public school, later a high school, whose management the *bourgeois* had confided to pensioned priests.
>
> Finally he is the only pupil left, the school ceases to exist, and the twelve-year-old boy is taken to Bromberg. There he undergoes seven years of drudgery in a Prussian high school, a school given over to false teaching and militarizing. After passing the college entrance examinations, his *wander-*

* *At that time, part of German Poland.—L. U.*

lust (which, while a boy, had carried him on a runaway trip to Bornholm and Denmark) takes him to France. He studies at the University of Grenoble and rambles about southern France and northern Italy.

The end of July, 1914, finds him at Lyons on his way to Paris. The German consul at Lyons, a man who possessed the same amount of vision as most German foreign representatives, quiets his disturbed fears (this is on the thirty-first of July) and advises him to proceed to Paris. That night he hears the shrill cry of the newsboys: "Declaration of War between Germany and Russia imminent." He leaves Lyons by the last train that goes to Geneva. On the way, he is arrested, freed, rearrested, freed again, and after an adventurous journey, reaches Switzerland a few minutes before the French frontier is closed. In Munich he reports as a volunteer, with the firm conviction that it is his duty to defend his "attacked fatherland." In the days in which he grows to be a soldier, he leaves the traditional sphere of the bourgeois, a departure with which he was acquainted when, in a newspaper article as a boy of thirteen, he sided with a pauper against the authorities, an action for which he was punished and dismissed from school.

He lives to see "the great Day!" but fights from the very first the hate and orgies of revenge of the journalistic and "literary" vipers. Thirteen months of service in the field. He believes in his duty—he murders, murders . . . and at last finds himself facing a heap of "French" and "German" corpses, in the Fôret des Prêtes. These corpses, in a ghastly embrace, seem to lift their stark fists in protest against a humanity which despoils itself, against a fate which gloats in the *danse macabre* of blinded nations.

He is convalescent, a penitent, yet laden with crime: a murderer whose hands can never again be clean.

He is discharged, invalided. He studies for a term in Munich. Slowly he finds himself. He is no longer weary, torn by a disgust of the age, and therefore shunning the events of the times. He has grown to be a rebel through and through.

He searches for comrades. He takes part in the "Kultur" congress at Burg Lauenstein, which the publisher Diedrichs has convened. He beholds the confusion, the cowardice, and the dejection of his seniors. He is in love with reality and, with angry words, censures those traitors to youth. He resolves to find revolutionary young blood. In the winter of 1917, he studies at Heidelberg and enjoys the privilege of being a guest at the house of Max Weber. (One of the few German bourgeois professors who was a politician. And a man of character—in Germany something even more significant!) He is invited to join a circle of students, young men and women, united by gloomy and uncertain impulses. They discuss the problems of the age; they all realize, with the full strength of their love of truth and justice, that discussion can bring no solution. His call to conspire against "the great Day" binds all these spirited youths. A cultural-political federation of German youth springs into being, its platform bears a naïve-socialistic, utopian-socialistic character. Fantastic ideas struggle toward materialization—the phalanx of German revolutionary youth is to unite with the revolutionary youth of the "enemy," end the war, build by itself the League of Nations. How to rouse the youth?

The faith of "the guileless fools" clings to the godlike potency of words. Appeals will assemble those holding like views. The writer plans to publish plays of Tolstoi and Landauer, of Barbusse's "Le Feu," of Frank's "Der Mensch ist gut," in cheap pamphlet form. Like a Don Quixote of 1917, furiously attacked by the Pan-German fraternities, the federation holds its own. The attention of the notorious news bureau of the General Staff is attracted. A few of the students who are members of the federation are conscripted without any examination. (Among them is Bernhard Schottlaender, who was foully murdered in Breslau in 1920 by followers of Kapp.) Austrian girl-students are forced to leave Germany.

The writer succeeds in escaping to Berlin.* Here he becomes acquainted with some kindred spirits. (Kurt Eisner is one of these.) He reads the political articles of the day and gains the, to him, staggering conviction that the German Government is not innocent of the outbreak of the war nor yet of its continuation—that the German people are being deceived. He makes a close study of the management of the war, its aims and purposes, and the path that leads to the proletariat lies clearer and clearer before him.

In January, 1918, he comes to Munich and takes part in the strike of the munitions-workers. Reclaimed workers, escaped from service at the front, employed at high wages, arose and fought for their European brothers in the field. Peace without any annexations, open or secret, the certainty of self-determination of all countries, including Germany—these were the slogans of the awakened proletariat. After Kurt Eisner's arrest on the first day of the strike, the workers elect the writer a member of the strike committee. He speaks at public meetings on the Theresienwiese, participates in the negotiations with the police commissioner which are

* *This is during the war, in 1917.—L. U.*

begun to secure Eisner's release, and at the end of the strike is arrested, charged with "attempted treason"! At the same time, he is again conscripted without a medical examination.

Months of scientific work in the military prison and the custody of the barracks. If, before this, he was a rebel from sentiment, he now becomes a revolutionary socialist through understanding. The drama "Wandlung" is created during walks in the dingy square of the prison yard.

The Revolution of November leads him to Munich. He is elected chairman of the Central Committee of Workers', Peasants', and Soldiers' Soviets, and takes part in the meetings of the Bavarian National Congress, the first German Soviet held in Bavaria. In March, 1919, the Independent Socialist Party elects him chairman. Although he himself is a Communist, he combats the proclamation of a Bavarian Soviet, because he believes that the time is not yet ripe for it. Inasmuch as a Soviet had already been spontaneously created in many Bavarian cities, however, he feels that it is not a proclamation which is necessary, but the understanding and mastery of existing conditions, and he accepts the election to enter the government of the Soviet Republic. In the first Soviet he is Chairman of the Central Committee; in the second, member of the Red Guard. Recognizing that Munich is cut off on all sides, realizing the disaster of a bloody defeat of the workers, he attempts to prepare a dissolution of the Soviet, the end of April. Without success. The revolutionary uprising, last rash attempt of a vanguard of workers to save the German November Revolution, is beaten.

A price of 10,000 marks is set on the writer's head. On June, 1919, he is arrested. On June 14th, 15th, 16th, he is brought before the Munich Court Martial. He is condemned to imprisonment in a fortress for five years.

Toller, student, soldier, worker, rebel, poet, and playwright—Herman Scheffauer calls him "the most dominant and flagrant genius hatched by the German Revolution"—was saved from the firing squad by his creative genius. At present (in 1923), he is serving the fourth year of his sentence—despite the efforts of Gerhart Hauptmann and others to have it commuted—and his four volumes have already made him one of the outstanding figures in Central European letters. "Man and the Masses," which has been a sensation wherever it has been presented, was preceded (and prepared for) by a drama related to it in intensity as well as theme. The earlier play was "Die Wandlung" (it translates itself inadequately into "The Transformation"), a man's journey *via* six "stations" which, in turn, are divided into thirteen pictures. "Die Wandlung" is an outraged protest against war—a protest that is both unrestrainedly bitter and deeply ecstatic. It is definitely expressionistic and undoubtedly autobiographic—a man's progress from the beginnings of war through its black hell to his own salvation. The play begins with a Prologue in which War Death (in steel helmet and a chestful of medals) and Civilian Death (in high silk hat and frock coat) meet on a field of graves to conduct their business; it ends, equally symbolically, with the destruction of a civic statue—"Our Victorious Nation"—and an anti-nationalist exhortation to the crowd before the church, an appeal to unite, to destroy the forces of destruction, to build only through love.

"Man and the Masses" takes up the theme where its forerunner left it. Here war is again the *motif;* but where in "Die Wandlung" it dominated the characters, in "Man and the Masses" it is no more than a sombre and intensely moving background. The struggle here is between the passions in man rather than between nations. Man as an individual against Man as a member of the community; Man as a part of the Mass alternately yielding to and repudiating the common impulses, the mob emotions of the Mass. This, in essence, is the spiritual conflict projected by Toller's characters. These characters are, as Toller has pointed out in his preface to the second edition, types rather than persons—only one (the Woman, Sonia Irene L.) is given a name; the rest are just so many figures (the Man, the Nameless One, the Companion, etc.), mouthpieces for elemental and clashing forces. It is a triple struggle in which the three chief protagonists are only symbols. The Man represents the State, the unquestioned faith in government as God, in law-imposing and law-obeying bodies. The Woman is the radical humanitarian; she not only questions the existing order, she challenges it; man, chained to the machine and almost destroyed by the systems of modern civilization, must be freed to find his destiny—and divinity—in communal labour! To the Nameless One, this is pretty, futile sentimentality. The Nameless One stands for ruthless Revolution; men are no more sacred to him than to the reactionary worshipper of the State; he, too, is willing to send thousands to their death for a Principle. Between these opposed but equally merciless antagonisms, the heroine is sacrificed. Hers is the spirit of a new Christ when, her rescue dependent on the death of a single enemy guard, she refuses to escape and cries: "A leader has the right to sacrifice no one but himself."

Although there are moments of personal poignance between the woman who has left her circle for the workers and her rigidly orthodox husband, the play is essentially a play of larger passions, in which the alternating scenes (the second, fourth, and sixth) are dream pictures. These scenes take place in the soul of the woman, distortions of fragments of scenes which have already taken place; vivid self-analyses, projections of her tortured mind. It is in these pictures that the dramatist suddenly lifts us to symbolic heights, mysterious, moving, unearthly.

This sense of unearthly space, of a half-dusky, half-dazzling limbo has been created not only by Toller but, as his significant "Letter to a Creative Producer" indicates, even more by the man who staged and directed the play. Those who saw the original production by Jurgen Fehling and his stage designer, Hans Strohbach, at the Berlin Volksbühne (September, 1921), have declared it one of the most memorable expressions of the new simplicity in the theatre. Realism is completely discarded. Light is used arbitrarily, changing suddenly to indicate the rapid changes of mood. Even the author's explicit directions for the "actual" scenes are thrown overboard. The first scene, for example, calls for a workman's tavern. On the whitewashed wall, pictures of heroes of the masses. But in the first scene, as Fehling and Strohbach produced it —and as Lee Simonson, following their lead, staged it for the Theatre Guild at the Garrick—there are none of these backgrounds and properties, no tavern, no walls, no portraits. There is only a platform with a few steps leading down into a seething darkness. "Upon this platform," to quote Kenneth Macgowan, "spotted out with three shafts of light, are the two men and the woman in the taut attitudes of wrestlers as they clasp hands, the woman in the middle." Throughout the play, this intensification of the emotional values is maintained. The voice of the mass rises out of crowded blackness ("Nothing like this voice, coming out of darkness in which faces vaguely begin to hover, has been imagined, much less attempted, in our theatre," writes Macgowan), lights shoot down upon phalanxes of workers, colours ray out like a fan, flashing and twisting in *macabre* turbulence. . . . Thus the most vital and spasmodic piece of expressionism has been interpreted on the stage.

II

Apart from these two dramas, Toller has established himself as poet as well as playwright. A sonnet sequence, entitled "Gedichte der Gefangenen" ("Poems of a Prisoner") appeared in 1921. Two choral works, "Tag des Proletariats" ("Day of the Proletariat") and "Requiem den erschossenen Brüdern" ("Requiem for Brothers who were shot") have also been published. In all of these, the one flaming impulse is manifest: the liberation of humanity from the chains of its material slavery. The cry continually ascends: "When will this heavy, stifling night be at an end?" Sometimes Toller's own reply is equally dark and doubtful——

We do not know. We only know that man
Goes armed against his brother. That no bridge can span
These separate streams of I and You. That no one sees
The way because of utter darkness. That we freeze.

At other times, the answer is more confident; his belief in the people is unshakable. "Perhaps," he writes, "only after man is crucified can he achieve resurrection and liberty."

Besides the preceding dramas and his purely poetic work, Toller is the author of "Die Maschinenstürmer" ("The Wreckers"—or, literally, "The Stormers of the Machine"), published and produced in 1922—an explosive tragedy which has for its background the Luddite riots, in Nottingham about 1815—and he has in preparation "Die Rache des Verhöhnten Liebhabers" ("The Revenge of the Scorned Lover") and "Eugen Hinkemann" ("Eugene Hinkemann"). "Die Rache des Verhöhnten Liebhabers" is Toller's single departure from his chosen subject. It is a glorified puppet play in two acts, suggested by a story of Cardinal Bandello (about 1550) and is gracefully erotic in character. Of "Eugen Hinkemann," which is a tragedy in three acts, Fritz Droop, Toller's annotator, writes: "With 'Eugen Hinkemann,' Toller returns to political drama. . . . I believe it is not only Toller's ripest work, but one of the most thrilling dramas of the last decade."

Although it is true that Toller's preoccupation with the sufferings of mankind motivates all he creates, it must not be inferred that he is a mere propagandist. He is, first of all, a poet, an emotional creator who is torn by his sympathy with both sides. He burns with one great cleansing flame but, as Scheffauer has said: "He offers his fire and brimstone in vessels shaped by his art."

III

A word as to Toller's idiom. Toller's style is a highly individualized one, abrupt, elliptical, and rich in unspoken overtones. It is, for the most part, a grave, sonorous speech continually broken up by a sharp and intense staccato; the tone wavers between that of irregular blank verse and an almost ecstatic prose. The translator, in an effort to maintain this flexibility, has had to compromise, sacrificing a syllable here, a nuance there. In spite of some of the sudden transitions, however, it seemed most important to preserve the pattern of this speech—a strange combination of elastic blank verse and *vers libre* interrupted by bursts of lyrical rhapsody. Many of the word arrangements in the original are Toller's own, and any weakness in verbal design should be laid, not only to the limitations of the two languages, but to the translator's own inadaptability.

It remains to say that—assuming the first person as I back toward the wings—I am grateful to Toller himself for much help, especially in the preparation of this preface, and to Lee Simonson and Lucy Wiener for many critical suggestions. I regret that, having listed Toller's other work in the original, I cannot append a complete English bibliography. However, for those further interested, there are three essays of importance: "The Drama on Fire," by Herman George Scheffauer (in *The Double Dealer*—a monthly magazine published at New Orleans—September, 1922), "The Machine-Stormers," also by Scheffauer (in *The Freeman*, January 17, 1923), and the chapter entitled "Masse-Mensch"(Man and the Masses) from the illuminating volume, "Continental Stagecraft," by Kenneth Macgowan and Robert Edmond Jones. My indebtedness is recorded if not discharged by this acknowledgment.

L. U.

New York City,
January, 1923.

The cast of the THEATRE GUILD PRODUCTION as originally presented at the GARRICK THEATRE, April 14, 1924

MAN AND THE MASSES

(MASSE MENSCH)

A tragedy of the Social Revolution—in seven scenes

By ERNST TOLLER

Translated by Louis Untermeyer

The production designed and directed by Lee Simonson

CHARACTERS (In order of appearance)

The Woman .... Blanche Yurka
The Man—Her Husband .... Ullrich Haupt
The Nameless One .... Jacob Ben-Ami
(*The Spirit of the Masses*)
The Companion (*a dream figure*) .... Arthur Hughes
First Banker .... A. P. Kaye
Second Banker .... William Franklin
Third Banker .... Erskine Sanford
Fourth Banker .... Leonard Loan
Fifth Banker .... Barry Jones
Sixth Banker .... Charles Tazewell
The Condemned One .... John McGovern
First Working Man .... Maurice McRae
Second Working Man .... Allyn Joslyn
Third Working Man .... Marling Chilton
Fourth Working Man .... Samuel Rosen
Fifth Working Man .... Robert Brodeur
A Working Woman .... Pauline Moore
An Officer .... Charles Tazewell
A Priest .... Erskine Sanford
First Woman Prisoner .... Zita Johann
Second Woman Prisoner .... Marietta Hyde
Messenger Boy .... Sidney Dexter
Chorus of Young Working Women .... Ethel Woodworth, Barbara Bruce, Pauline Moore, Betsy Hatch, Phoebe Kaye, Gladys Pabst, Jeanne Powers, Zita Johann, Barbara Benedict, Barbara Kitson

Chorus of Young Working Men .... Charles Freeman, Leonard Loan, Allyn Joslyn, Samuel Rosen, Robert Brodeur, Maurice McRae, George Bratt, George Chiles, Marling Chilton, Harry McKenna, Albert Hecht, John Crump.
Chorus of Agricultural Workers .... John McGovern, Marietta Hyde, Jessie Tharp, George Stehli, Charles Tazewell.

Brokers, Guards, Soldiers, Convicts, and Shadows.

Stage Manager: Jo Mielziner

Assistant Stage Managers: Emanuel Schrader, Barbara Kitson

MAN AND THE MASSES is a play of the Communist Revolt. Although it was written by an arden Communist, it is really a poet's profound questioning of revolution. Its theme is the inevitably tragic nature of the conflict between man, the individual, and the needs of the mass. The protagonist is a woman profoundly convinced that no cause can be really won if it is won at the price of war and bloodshed.

The second, fourth, and fifth scenes take place in the woman's mind, projecting through a dream medium her horror of capitalistic control, of proletarian warfare, and her pity for its victims.

SYNOPSIS OF SCENES

Scene I. A Working Man's Hall on the Eve of the Revolution. The Husband, symbolizing the State, tries to dissuade the Woman from the Communist leadership she has assumed.

Scene II. A Dream Scene. A grotesque and distorted stock exchange projected in the Woman's mind, where the bankers "fatten on human flesh," and national victories and disasters are only significant as they affect the fluctuations of stocks and bonds. The husband appears as the recorder of sales.

Scene III. A Meeting Hall of the Revolutionists. The Woman, symbolizing the individual, pleads for a bloodless strike, as against the Nameless One, who represents Mass, crying for revolution.

Scene IV. A Dream Scene, projected by the Woman's mind, tortured at having consented to revolution, and haunted by the fear that she may ultimately bring harm to her husband. The scene is a stockade, where the workers and their prisoners are stirred by the Nameless One to a macabre dance. The Husband is brought in by the revolutionists to be shot, a fate which many of their number have already suffered at the hands of the bourgeoisie. The Woman in her dream intercedes for her husband's life.

Scene V. The Meeting Hall of the Revolutionists, in which the workers, suffering defeat, make a last stand against the overwhelming power of the state.

Scene VI. A Dream Scene. The Woman's mind, tortured by the horrors of the revolution, has assumed the guilt and suffering for the masses and is haunted by the spirits of the prisoners and the bankers. Encaged in her doubts, her questioning soul finally lifts itself from a sense of individual responsibility to the realization of a cosmic guilt, and she accuses God in her despair.

Scene VII. A Prison. The Woman's husband comes to her with a hope of pardon, and the assurance of his belief in her innocence, which she rejects because it is motivated by the change in public opinion. Next the priest comes to her, and she upholds her faith in the indestructible good of human nature against the church's belief in man's inherent evil. In a final scene the Nameless One offers her liberation at the expense of the death of one of the prison guards, which she—symbolizing the ultimate pacifistic spirit, standing between the State, which is War, and the Nameless One, who is Revolution—rejects, because she believes that no cause can ever be rightly won at the cost of human life. As she goes to her death, two of the starving workers find themselves quarrelling over her few possessions, only to be wakened to the significance of their act by the shots of the firing squad.

There will be intermissions of ten minutes between scenes 3 and 4,
and between scenes 5 and 6.

Assistant in Production: Philip Loeb

The Guild acknowledges the assistance of Louise Gifford in training the chorus movements

The THEATRE GUILD, Inc.

Board of Managers

Theresa Helburn	Philip Moeller	Maurice Wertheim
Lawrence Langner	Lee Simonson	Helen Westley

Executive Director: Theresa Helburn

Scenic Director	*Play Reading Dept.*	*Business Manager*
Lee Simonson	Courtenay Lemon	Warren P. Munsell
Technical Director	*Press Representative*	*Stage Manager*
Carolyn Hancock	Ruth Benedict	Robert L. Cook

Address communications to the Theatre Guild, Inc., 65 West 35th Street, New York City

LIST OF ILLUSTRATIONS

MAN AND THE MASSES

FIRST PICTURE

MAN AND THE MASSES

FIRST PICTURE

[*Back room of a workmen's tavern. On the white-washed wall are pictures of soldiers' councils and heroes of the masses. In the centre of the room, a crude table around which a* WOMAN *and several* WORKMEN *are sitting.*]

FIRST WORKMAN

Hand-bills have been distributed
In the great convention hall.
To-morrow the factories will close early.
The masses seethe.
To-morrow—the decision.
Are you ready, comrade?

THE WOMAN

I am.
Strength grows with every breath—
How I have longed for this hour,
Where the heart's blood finds words.

And words grow into deeds!
Impotence shook me often—and I clenched
My hands in shame and agony and fury.
When filthy papers trumpet "Victory,"
A million hands take hold of me
And cry:
"You are guilty of our death!"
Yes, every horse with shivering, foaming flanks,
Accuses me in silence . . . accuses me.—
Yet, since I sound the final call to-morrow,
There, where my conscience flames up in the hall,
Shall I not be the one to proclaim the strike?
Mankind cries, Strike! Nature cries, Strike!
The river hisses, Strike!
Even the dog, it seems, barks for it as he leaps
When I come home. . . .
I feel it in each vein. The masses rise,
Free of red tape, of webs spun out
By well-fed gentlemen around green tables.
Armies of mankind, with overpowering purpose,
Will build a structure of peace to unknown heights.
The red flag . . . flag of bright beginnings . . .
Banner of daybreak . . .
Who will lead with it?

SECOND WORKMAN

You! They follow you!

[*Silence flickers.*]

THE WOMAN

Can we be sure no one has talked?
You think the police have had no information?
Suppose the soldiers form a chain around the hall?

FIRST WORKMAN

The police know nothing. And if they do,
They never know our real intentions.
When once the masses can possess the hall
They'll make a raging flood that no police
Can tame into a plashing, park-like fountain.
Besides, the police won't dare to interfere,
Broken ranks have eaten up their sense of power.
The regiments, moreover, are on our side—
Councils of soldiers everywhere!
To-morrow—comrade—the decision!

[*A knock.*]

Betrayed!

SECOND WORKMAN

They must not find you.

FIRST WORKMAN

Only one door.

SECOND WORKMAN

Through the window!

FIRST WORKMAN

The window opens on an air-shaft.

THE WOMAN

And the struggle so near . . .

[*A louder knocking. The door is opened. The* MAN, *his coat-collar pulled up, comes in, looks about him quickly, and raises his derby.*]

THE WOMAN

A—friend . . . And there's no danger . . .
You come to me;
You find me.

THE MAN

Good evening.
[*Softly*]:
Please don't introduce me.
May I speak with you?

THE WOMAN (*to the others*)

Comrades . . .

THE WORKMEN

Good-night.
Until to-morrow.

[*Exeunt.*]

THE WOMAN

Good-night; until to-morrow.

THE MAN

I must make it clear,
I did not come to help you.

THE WOMAN

Forgive the dream that blossomed for a moment.

THE MAN

My honour's threatened—that is why I'm here.

THE WOMAN

And I'm the cause? How strange . . .
Honour, you say. Honour of the bourgeois class?
And were there tongues of disapproval?
Did the outraged majority
Threaten to bar you from its sacred ranks?

THE MAN

Please don't be flippant.
Consideration for others—an emotion to which you
are a stranger—
Is law for me.
For me the strictest code of honour still survives.

THE WOMAN

To stamp its pattern on you.

THE MAN

Self-control implies subordination.
We must submit . . .
Your thoughts are not upon my words.

THE WOMAN

I see your eyes.

THE MAN

Don't disconcert me.

THE WOMAN

You . . . You . . .

THE MAN

To come to the point,
You must give up your work.

THE WOMAN

You . . .

THE MAN

The desire for social service—
Laudable, I'll grant—

Can be fulfilled in our own circle.
Let's say, a home for illegitimate children.
Ideas are the foundation of all work,
Proof of the very culture you deride.
Even your new-found friends, your so-called comrades,
Despise the unmarried mother.

THE WOMAN

Go on . . . go on . . .

THE MAN

You are not free to act as you may choose.

THE WOMAN

I am free . . .

THE MAN

I think I may assume some personal consideration,
A certain measure of respect—
If not from conviction, then for appearances.

THE WOMAN

I have respect for nothing but my work.
That work commands me; that is all I serve.

THE MAN

Let's analyze you:
A wish for a new sort of service prompts your actions—

A wish born of a conflict of emotions.
I am, you understand, far from implying
That this wish springs from any base desires.

THE WOMAN

How you can wound me with your words . . .
Tell me, have you ever seen the pictures of Madonnas
In peasants' houses?
Swords pierce the breast, the heart bleeds great dark tears.
Those gaudy, hideous, terribly moving prints . . .
So common—and so great . . .
You . . . you . . .
You speak of desires?
I know—a chasm yawns between us . . .
But it was not a whim that made me turn,
No *wish* to change my way of living.
It was a *need* . . . Need of my very self,
Need of the darkest depths of my existence.
Need alters us, I tell you, need changes us.
Not moods or spells or fits of boredom,
But need—the need to be a human being.

THE MAN

Need? Have you the right
To speak of need?

THE WOMAN

You . . . my husband . . . do not torture me . . .
Now I hold your head . . .
Now I kiss your eyes . . .
You . . .
Say no more . . .

THE MAN

To hurt you was the last thing I intended . . .
But this place . . .
Can any one overhear us?

THE WOMAN

Suppose a comrade does hear us?
They have understanding even though they lack your "code of honour."
Oh, if you only understood them,
If you could only get a breath of their great need.
Need . . . which is—which must be . . . ours!
You—you have lowered them . . .
And, in lowering them, you have debased yourself;
You have become your own executioner . . .
I do not want the pity in your eyes!
I'm not neurotic,
Not the least bit sentimental.

And since I'm not, I belong to them.
Oh, those miserable little hours you put aside
For social betterment—
A soothing syrup for your pity and weakness.
Many a comrade feels ashamed for you,
When they don't . . . laugh at you . . .
As I am laughing.

THE MAN

So—you may as well know everything.
They know about you—the authorities.
I took an oath of loyalty to the State.
The chief detective has been informed . . .
Otherwise, progress in my career would be impossible.

THE WOMAN

And . . . ?

THE MAN

I tell you this,
Regardless of the consequences,
Which, you may be sure,
Affect me, too,
Especially since you would harm both the career
Of your husband and the welfare of the State . . .
You help the enemy within our gates.
This gives me grounds for a divorce.

THE WOMAN

Of course . . . if I have harmed you,
If I have stood in your way . . .

THE MAN

There still is time.

THE WOMAN

Then, of course,
Then . . . I am prepared . . .
I accept the blame . . .
You need not fear, the trial will not harm you.
You . . .
You . . . my arms stretch out to you
With hungry need.
You . . . my blood swells to you . . .
See—I am a withered leaf without you.
You are the dew that makes me blossom.
You are the storm whose April strength
Flings flaming torches in my thirsty veins. . . .
There were warm nights . . . calls of young boys
in spring
Exulting in the vigour of their blood. . . .
Take me away to meadows, fields, or woodlands;
Meekly will I bow down and kiss your eyes. . . .
I know I will be very weak
Without you . . . unbelievably. . . .

[*Short pause.*]

Forgive me—I was weak just now.
I see the situation clearly; I understand your action.
Nevertheless—to-morrow I appear before the masses—
To-morrow I speak to them.
To-morrow I attack the State, to which you swore allegiance,
Tearing the old mask from its murderous face.

THE MAN

Your act is treason to the State.

THE WOMAN

Your State makes war;
Your State betrays the people!
Your State exploits, grinds down
And robs the people of their rights!

THE MAN

The State is holy. . . . War insures its life.
Peace is a phantom of weak minds.
War is nothing but an interrupted armistice,
In which the State continually lives,
Constantly threatened by its foes without
And enemies within.

THE WOMAN

How can a body live that's eaten up by plague
And burned by fire?

Have you seen the naked body of the State?
Have you seen the worms that feed upon it?
Have you seen the stock exchanges, the financiers
That gorge themselves with human flesh?
You have not seen it. . . . You have sworn allegiance to the State;
You do your duty and your conscience is quieted.

THE MAN

And this decision is your last word?

THE WOMAN

My last word.

THE MAN

Good-night!

THE WOMAN

Good-night!

[*As the* MAN *starts to go:*]

May I go with you?
To-night for the last time . . .
Or am I shameless?
Or am I shameless . . .
Shameless in my desire? . . .
[*The* WOMAN *follows the* MAN. *The stage darkens.*]

SECOND PICTURE

Setting by Lee Simonson *Photograph by Francis Bruguiere*

Scene II from The Theatre Guild Production

SECOND PICTURE

(DREAM-PICTURE)

[*A room of the stock exchange. At the desk, a* CLERK; *about him* BANKERS *and* BROKERS. *The* CLERK *has the face of the man of the first scene.*]

CLERK

Recorded.

FIRST BANKER

Munition works,
Three-fifty.

SECOND BANKER

I offer
Four hundred.

THIRD BANKER

Four hundred
Offered.

[*The* FOURTH BANKER *draws the* THIRD BANKER *toward the front. In the background there is the murmur of bidders and sellers.*]

FOURTH BANKER (*to the* THIRD BANKER)

Did you hear?
Retreat necessary.

Great offensive
Can't succeed.

THIRD BANKER

Reserves?

FOURTH BANKER

Human material
Running poor.

THIRD BANKER

Food inadequate?

FOURTH BANKER

That also.
Although
Professor Ude
Thinks
That rye
Ground down
With ninety-five per cent. of chaff
Will make
A food for epicures.

THIRD BANKER

The leaders?

FOURTH BANKER

Splendid.

THIRD BANKER

Not enough alcohol?

FOURTH BANKER

Distilleries
Working
Overtime.

THIRD BANKER

What's wrong?

FOURTH BANKER

The General
Has called ninety-three professors
To headquarters.
Also our expert,
Councillor Glubor.
There'll be results.

THIRD BANKER

They are?

FOURTH BANKER

Not to be discussed
In bourgeois circles.

THIRD BANKER

Are the soldiers weakened
By love of man?

And independent
Of the exchange.

THIRD BANKER

And well financed?

FOURTH BANKER

Syndicate of the largest banks
Will underwrite it.

THIRD BANKER

The profit?
Dividends?

FOURTH BANKER

Will be divided regularly.

THIRD BANKER

The form of the enterprise sounds good.
But what's the scheme?

FOURTH BANKER

We'll camouflage and call it
Recreation Home:
A Place to Strengthen the Desire to Win!
The real thing:
National brothels.

THIRD BANKER

Magnificent!
I subscribe one hundred thousand.
Just one more question,
Who regulates the amount of time,
Energy to be spent, et cetera?

FOURTH BANKER

Experienced generals.
They know
The standard regulations.

THIRD BANKER

The plan
Drawn up yet?

FOURTH BANKER

To be regulated,
As I just said.
Three prices.
Three divisions.
Brothel for officers:
Stay there all night.
Brothel for corporals:
One hour.
Brothel for privates:
Fifteen minutes.

THIRD BANKER

Thanks.
When does the market open?

FOURTH BANKER

Any minute.
[*Noise in the background.* THIRD *and* FOURTH BANKER *go to the rear.*]

THE CLERK

New issue ready:
National bonds,
War Recreation Home
Ltd.

FIRST BANKER

I have no order to buy.

SECOND BANKER

The dividend does not tempt me.

THIRD BANKER

I subscribe to one hundred thousand
At par.

THE CLERK

Recorded.

FOURTH BANKER

Same here.

FIRST BANKER (*to the* SECOND BANKER)

The cool one's buying. . . .
What do you think?

SECOND BANKER

Just got a telegram:
The drive on the West front
Has been lost. . . .

FIRST BANKER

Gentlemen,
The drive on the West front has been lost.

[*Cries, screams, shrieks.*]

VOICES

Lost!

A VOICE

I offer
Munition works
At one-fifty.

A VOICE

I offer
Liquid Flame Trust.

A Voice

I offer
War Prayer-Book, Ltd.

A Voice

Offer
Poison-Gas Works.

A Voice

Offer
War loans.

Third Banker

I'll take another
One hundred thousand.

A Voice

What?
When prices are tumbling?

A Voice

Who said we had lost the drive?

A Voice

Is the rumour true?
Or just a trick to get control of the market?
The cool one
Has bought his second hundred thousand.

SECOND BANKER

Something's wrong!
Switch my order!
I buy—
One-fifty.

A VOICE

I bid
Two hundred.

A VOICE

I buy
Three hundred.

A VOICE

Who bids?
Four hundred?
I buy.

THE CLERK

Recorded.

FOURTH BANKER (*to the* THIRD BANKER)

The old fox has guessed . . .

THIRD BANKER

Excuse the question.
Has our most important method
Been saved?

FOURTH BANKER

How can you even ask that?
Mechanics of life
Are so simple—
There was a leak . . .
It is discovered
And stopped at once.
A rise
Or a fall to-day
Means nothing.
The important thing
Is to keep our machinery going.
And so it follows
The system is safe.

THE CLERK

Recorded.
[*The* COMPANION *enters. His face is a composite of the features of death and the most radiant life. He leads the* WOMAN.]

THE COMPANION

Gentlemen,
You're ordering too quickly.
"Blood—and the System!"
"Man—and the System!"
You cannot unite them.

One stamp of the foot
And your whole mechanism
Is broken
Like a child's toy.
Look out!

[*To the* WOMAN:]

Speak to them!

THE WOMAN (*quietly*)

Gentlemen:
Human beings . . .
I say it again:
Human beings!

[*The* COMPANION *and the* WOMAN *fade. Sudden silence.*]

THIRD BANKER

You hear?
A disaster in the mines.
Seems
People are in distress.

FOURTH BANKER

I have an idea:
A Charity Festival.
Dance
On the floor of the stock exchange.

Dance
To aid the suffering.
Help
The unfortunates.
If it's convenient,
A little dance.
Gentlemen,
I contribute
One bond
War Recreation Home
Ltd.

A VOICE

How about women?

FOURTH BANKER

As many as you want.
Someone tell the doorman:
Five hundred
Gay
Young girls
Wanted here!
Meanwhile . . .

THE BANKERS

We donate!
We dance!

Help
The unfortunates!
[*Music of clinking gold-pieces. The* BANKERS *in their high silk hats dance a fox-trot around the exchange. The stage darkens.*]

THIRD PICTURE

THIRD PICTURE

[*The stage remains dark.*]

CHORUS OF THE MASSES (*as from a vast distance*)

We who are huddled for ever
In cañons of steel, cramped under cliffs of houses,
We who are delivered up
To the mockery of the machine,
We whose features are lost in a night of tears,
We, torn for ever from our mothers,
Out of the depths of factories, we cry to you:
When shall we, living, know the love of life?
When shall we, working, feel the joy of labour?
When shall deliverance come?

[*The stage becomes light. A great hall. On the platform a long narrow table. At the left, the* WOMAN *is sitting. In the room,* WORKING MEN *and* WORKING WOMEN *are packed closely together.*]

GROUP OF YOUNG WORKING GIRLS

And struggle breeds new struggles!
No compromising with these masters,

No loose agreements, feeble compacts.
Give orders to a group of comrades:
Dynamite in the machines!
To-morrow factories will explode into the air.
Machinery herds us all like beasts in stockyards,
Machinery clamps us in its metal vise,
Machinery pounds our bodies day by day
And turns us into rivets . . . screws . . .
Screws . . . three millimeters . . . screws
. . . five millimeters,
Withers our eyes, eats up our fingers,
While bodies go on living . . .
Down with the factories! Down with machinery!

SCATTERED CRIES IN THE HALL

Down with the factories! Down with machinery!

THE WOMAN

Once when I was blind, and felt the rods
Of engines pierce me and machines suck up my blood,
I, too, cried your despairing cry. . . .
It is a dream that limits your own vision,
A dream of children, frightened by the night.
For, see—this is the twentieth century.
We must realize
The factory cannot be wiped out.
Take all the dynamite on earth,

And, in one night, blast all the factories,
By next spring, they will rise again
To live more terribly than ever.
Factories must no longer be the master,
And man the raw material.
Factories must be our servants,
Helping to make a richer life.
The soul of man must master factories.

GROUP OF YOUNG WORKMEN

Let them and us be destroyed together!
See how our words rush to revenge and fury.
The masters live in palaces;
Our brothers rot in filthy trenches.
Somewhere there's lively pleasure, dances, songs—
At night we read of them and grind our teeth!
And longing burns in us for light and knowledge. . . .
They took this holy thing
And it turned horrible.
Sometimes, but rarely, it shines out at us
In the theatre,
And it is sweet . . . and clean . . . and always mocking!
In school their hatred cheated us of youth,
In schoolrooms they destroyed our souls.
Nothing but need makes us cry out. . . .
What are we to-day?
We will not wait!

Group of Agricultural Labourers

They turned us away from our mother earth.
These rich men buy up land as they buy street girls,
Amuse themselves with her, the holy mother,
And toss our raw flesh into munition plants.
But we grow sick, uprooted from our soil,
The unhappy cities sour us, break our strength.
We want the land!
The land for everybody!

Crowd in the Hall

The land for everybody!

The Woman

I went through the slums.
Gray rain dripped from dirty roofs;
Fungus sprouted from mouldy walls.
And in one room there sat an invalid
Who stuttered, "We were better off out there. . . .
Here we live in a pig pen . . .
Isn't it true . . . in a pig pen?"
A shamefaced smile slipped from his eyes.
And his shame shamed me. . . .
Brothers, do you want to know the way out?
There's one way left us weaklings,
For us who hate all war.

Strike! No more contracts, compromises.
Let our answer be, Strike!
We weak ones will become as strong as granite,
No weapon made can hope to conquer us.
Call to our mute battalions!
Summon our silent armies!
I cry, Strike!
Hear me:
I cry, Strike!
Moloch has fattened on our bodies
For six long years.
Pregnant women collapse upon the streets,
So starved they cannot even carry
The burden of the unborn.
Want stares at you in your homes;
Pestilence and madness glare at you,
And hunger, festering hunger. . . .
But there—look over there!
The bankers spend themselves in bacchanalia;
Champagne drowns every hard-fought victory;
Lust leaps and license stirs the dance
Around the golden altars.
And at the front?
Can you see the withered faces of your brothers?
Feel their bodies
Clammy in the fog and frost
Of twilight?
Smell the breath of that decay?

Hear their cries? I ask you.
Hear them calling?
"Brothers, we turn to you!
We, chained to the flanks of cannon,
We helpless ones,
We cry to you:
Help! Be our saviours!
You—be our rescue!
Hear me. I cry, Strike!
Whoever again eats munition wages
Betrays his brother.
What did I say—betrays?
He *kills* his brother.
And you, you women!
Do you know the story of those wives
Who remain barren
Because they helped forge deadly weapons?
Think of your men out there!
I cry, Strike!

CROWD IN THE HALL

We cry, Strike!
We cry
STRIKE!
[*Out of the crowd in the hall, the* NAMELESS ONE *emerges. He hurries to the platform, placing himself to the right of the table.*]

The Nameless One

The man who wants to build a bridge
Must pay attention to the pillars.
A strike to-day is a hasty bridge without supports.
We must have more than just a strike. . . .
Let's grant the thing's successful.
Suppose your strike forces them to a peace,
It is not Peace you've won—you've made *a* peace.
Instead of peace, you have a pause. That's all.
War must be stopped entirely,
Once and for all time.
But first, one final, desperate battle!
What will you gain if you halt this one struggle?
The peace that you create
Will leave your situation as it is.
On one hand, a false peace and old conditions.
On the other, a swift war and new conditions!
You fools, break down foundations;
Break the foundations, I tell you!
Then let the flood of your power wash away
The mouldering structure
Which only gold chains
Keep from falling apart.
Let us build a system under which we can live.
The factories belong to all the workers
And not to old man Capital.
The time has passed when, on our burdened backs,

He looked around with greedy eyes
For foreign treasures,
And planned fresh wars, enslaved an alien people,
Compelled the lying tongues of newspapers to scream:
"The Fatherland! All for the Fatherland!"
While underneath it rang the real refrain:
"For me! For me!"
That time has passed!
The masses of all nations have one cry:
The factories belong to all the workers!
All power to the workers!
All for us all!
I cry for more than Strike!
I cry, War!
I cry, Revolution!
Our enemy up there won't pay attention
To any pretty speeches.
Force against force!
Violence! . . . Violence!

A Voice

Arms!

The Nameless One

Yes, arms are all we need!
Go out and get them!
Storm the city hall!
The battle cry: Victory!

THE WOMAN

Hear me!
I must . . .

THE NAMELESS ONE

Quiet yourself, comrade.
Frantic appeals, clasped hands, and tearful prayers
Produce no children.
Consumptives can't get well on watered soup.
You have to use an axe to chop down trees.

THE WOMAN

Hear me . . .
I do not want fresh murders.

THE NAMELESS ONE

Silence, comrade.
What can you know?
You suffer our distress, I grant you that.
But have you worked ten hours in the mines,
A homeless child in blind, enormous rooms;
Ten hours in the mines—and the dark hut at evening? . . .
That is how day comes daily to the workers.
You are not one of them.
I am the Mass!
The Mass knows its own future.
The Mass is destiny!

A VOICE

Is destiny . . .

THE WOMAN

But think a moment,
Mass is powerless.
Mass is weak.

THE NAMELESS ONE

How little do you realize the truth!
Mass is leader!
Mass is strength!

CROWD IN THE HALL

Is strength!

THE WOMAN

Emotion pulls me toward the darkness
But all my conscience cries out, No!

THE NAMELESS ONE

Keep silent, comrade!
The cause demands it.
What does one person matter?
His feelings? or his conscience?
Only the Mass must count!
Just think of it: a single bloody battle

And then, eternal peace.
No empty peace, a mask of mockery,
Hiding the face of war,
War of the strong against the weak,
War of exploiters, war of greed.
Think of it: the end of misery!
Think of it: crime a half-remembered fable!
It is the dawn of freedom for all people! . . .
You think I reckon lightly?
It is no longer a matter of choice.
War's a necessity for us.
Your advice means discord.
For the sake of the cause,
Keep silent.

THE WOMAN

You . . . are . . . Mass.
You . . . are . . . right.

THE NAMELESS ONE

Beat in the pillars of the bridge, O comrades!
Drive over everyone who stands in our way.
Mass is action!

CROWD IN THE HALL (*as they storm out*)

Action!

[*The stage darkens.*]

FOURTH PICTURE

Setting by Lee Simonson *Photograph by Francis Bruguiere*

Scene IV from The Theatre Guild Production

FOURTH PICTURE

(DREAM-PICTURE)

[*A court with a high wall is suggested. On the ground in the middle of the court, a lantern which gives a miserable light.* WORKER GUARDS *suddenly emerge from the corners of the court.*]

FIRST GUARD (*sings*)

My mother
Bore me
In the mud of a trench.
Lalala la,
Hm, Hm.

SECOND GUARD

My father
Lost me
In a brawl with a wench.

ALL THE GUARDS

Lalala la,
Hm, Hm.

THIRD GUARD

Three years
I breathed
In the prison stench.

ALL THE GUARDS

Lalala la,
Hm, Hm.
[*With silent, ghostly steps, the* NAMELESS ONE *appears from somewhere. He stands near the lantern.*]

FIRST GUARD

Dear father
Forgot
To pay mother's fee.

ALL THE GUARDS

Lalala la,
Hm, Hm.

SECOND GUARD

Poor mother
Never
Gave anything free.

ALL THE GUARDS

Lalala la,
Hm, Hm.

THIRD GUARD

I troubled
The goddam
Bourgeoisie!

ALL THE GUARDS

Lalala la,
Hm, Hm.

THE NAMELESS ONE

Come, dance!
I'll play for you.

THE GUARDS

Halt!
Who are you?

THE NAMELESS ONE

Did I ask your names,
Nameless ones?

THE GUARDS

The password?

THE NAMELESS ONE

Mass is nameless!

ONE OF THE GUARDS

Is nameless.
He's one of us.

THE NAMELESS ONE

I'll play for you,
I, who announce
The great decision.

[*The* NAMELESS ONE *begins to play a harmonica. The rhythms of his tune are alternately rousing, swaying, and lascivious, then ponderous and stormy. A* CONDEMNED MAN, *a rope around his neck, steps out of the dark.*]

THE CONDEMNED MAN

In the name
Of those condemned to die,
We beg a final
Favour:
Let us join the dance.
The dance is the very centre
Of things.
Life, born of the dance,
Urges and runs
To the dance;
To the dance of desire,
To whirling Time
And its dance of death.

THE GUARDS

One should always
Grant the condemned

Their last request:
Invited.

THE NAMELESS ONE

Come, then!
One is as good as another.

THE CONDEMNED MAN (*calls in the darkness*)

All those
Condemned to death,
Step up!
The last dance!
Let the waiting coffins
Wait.

[*All the* CONDEMNED, *with ropes around their necks, step out of the darkness.* GUARDS *and the* CONDEMNED *dance about the* NAMELESS ONE.]

THE GUARDS (*singing*)

In the mud of a trench . . .

[*They dance on. After a short pause:*]

In a brawl with a wench . . .

[*They dance on. After a short pause:*]

In the prison stench . . .

[*They dance on.*]

[*The* NAMELESS ONE *breaks off suddenly. Prostitutes and those condemned to die run off to the dark corners of the court. Night swallows them up.*

THE GUARDS *strike a posture. Silence surrounds the* NAMELESS ONE. *The* COMPANION, *in the guise of a guard, glides through the wall. He holds a woman, who has the face of the woman of the preceding scenes, close to him.*]

THE COMPANION

The journey
Is difficult.
The result
Repays your trouble.
Look there—
The drama
Is about to begin.
If the impulse tempts you,
Act with it.

[*A* GUARD *brings in a* PRISONER *who has the features of the* MAN *and leads him to the* NAMELESS ONE.]

THE NAMELESS ONE

Condemned
By the tribunal?

A GUARD

He brought death
Upon himself.
He shot at us.

THE PRISONER

Death?

THE NAMELESS ONE

It frightens you?
Listen:
Guard! Answer me.
Who taught us
Capital punishment?
Who gave us weapons?
Who said "Hero" and "noble deed"?
Who glorified violence?

THE GUARDS

Schools.
Barracks.
War.
Always.

THE NAMELESS ONE

Force . . . violence and force.
Why did you shoot?

THE PRISONER

I swore
To protect the State.

THE NAMELESS ONE

You die
For your convictions.

THE GUARDS

To the wall with him!

THE NAMELESS ONE

Guns loaded?

THE GUARDS

Loaded.

THE PRISONER (*against the wall*)

Life!
Life!

[*The* WOMAN *tears herself from the* COMPANION.]

THE WOMAN

Don't shoot!
There stands my husband.
Forgive him
As I, too, humbly, forgive him.
Forgiveness is so strong
And far beyond all struggles.

THE NAMELESS ONE

Do they forgive
Us?

THE WOMAN

Do they struggle
For the people?

Do they fight
For humanity?

THE NAMELESS ONE

The Mass counts.

THE GUARDS

To the wall!

A GUARD

Forgiveness is cowardice.
Yesterday I escaped
From the enemy over there.
They stood me up against the wall,
My body covered with bruises.
Next to me the man
Who was to murder me.
I had to dig
My grave
With my own hands.
In front of us
The photographer,
Eager to etch
Murder
On his plates.
I say, to hell with the Revolution
If it lets
Those grinning murderers over there

Make monkeys of us.
I say,
To hell with the Revolution!

THE GUARDS

To the wall!
[*The face of the* PRISONER *changes to that of one of the* GUARDS. *The* WOMAN *speaks to the* GUARD *who has just finished.*]

THE WOMAN

Yesterday they stood you
Against the wall.
Now you are standing
Against the wall again.
That is you
Who are standing there
Against the wall to-day.
Man—
You are he.
Recognize yourself—
You are man.

A GUARD

The Mass counts.

THE WOMAN

The Man counts.

ALL THE GUARDS

The Mass counts!

THE WOMAN (*despairingly*)

I give
Myself . . .
All of myself . . . to you . . .

[*The* GUARDS *laugh lewdly.*]

THE WOMAN (*placing herself next to the* MAN)

Shoot then!
I give up. . . .
I am so tired . . .

[*The stage darkens.*]

FIFTH PICTURE

Setting by Lee Simonson *Photograph by Francis Bruguiere*

Scene V from The Theatre Guild Production

FIFTH PICTURE

[*The hall. Gray dawn crawls through the windows. The platform is illuminated with a gloomy light. The* WOMAN *sits at the left of the long table, the* NAMELESS ONE *at the right.* WORKER GUARDS *at the doors of the hall. In the hall, isolated* WORKMEN *and* WORKWOMEN *huddle about tables.*]

THE WOMAN

Has any news come within the last hour?
Forgive me, comrade, I slept.

THE NAMELESS ONE

Report crowds upon report.
War is war;
A bloody game and one to be played coolly.
Before midnight we occupied the station.
At one o'clock we lost it.
Detachments are moving up now
For a fresh assault.
The post-office is in our hands.
At this very moment

Telegrams are being sent to the nations,
Telling them of our work.

THE WOMAN

Work! What a holy word!

THE NAMELESS ONE

A holy word, comrade!
It calls for more than speeches and a warm heart,
It calls for implements of steel,
It calls for ruthless war.
[*A second's flickering silence in the hall.*]

THE WOMAN

Comrade, for all you say, I cannot be convinced.
To fight with weapons is to win through force.

THE NAMELESS ONE

Mental weapons are also a force in battle.
Words can be murderers.—
Don't be so startled, comrade.
I deal in naked truths.
Why, if I thought as you, I'd be a monk
Walking some cloister in eternal silence.
[*Silence seems to sink heavily upon the hall.* FIRST WORKMAN *enters.*]

FIRST WORKMAN

I bring news.
We advanced three times against the station.
The place is thick with dead.
Damn them, they're well fortified,
Supplied with every kind of weapon,
Flame-throwers, hand-grenades, poison gas.

THE NAMELESS ONE

You advanced three times.
And the fourth time?

FIRST WORKMAN

We did not advance four times.
The others charged on us.

THE NAMELESS ONE

You held them.
Do you need support?

FIRST WORKMAN

We have been scattered.

THE NAMELESS ONE

Reverses were to be expected.
Attention! Go to the thirteenth district;

The reserves are there.
Go—hurry!

[*The* WORKMAN *goes.*]

THE WOMAN

He spoke of dead.
Many hundreds.
Yesterday I cried out against all war—
And to-day . . . I let them kill;
I let brothers be flung to death.

THE NAMELESS ONE

Your vision is not clear.
In yesterday's war we fought as slaves.

THE WOMAN

And to-day?

THE NAMELESS ONE

To-day in battle we are free.

[*Fevered silence.*]

THE WOMAN

In both wars . . . human beings . . .
In both wars . . . human beings . . .

[*Silence reels.* SECOND WORKMAN *stumbles in.*]

SECOND WORKMAN

The post-office is lost!
Our men are retreating!
The enemy gives no quarter.
Any one captured is shot!

[FIRST WORKMAN *rushes in.*]

FIRST WORKMAN

I come from the thirteenth district.
Struggle is useless.
The streets are closed.
The district has surrendered.
They're giving up their weapons.

THIRD WORKMAN

The city's lost!
The work has failed.

THE WOMAN

It had to fail . . .

THE NAMELESS ONE

Once more, keep silent, comrade!
Our work is not a failure.
If we were not strong enough to-day,
To-morrow there'll be fresh battalions.

FOURTH WORKMAN (*crying in the hall*)

They're coming out against us!
O terrible slaughter!
They shot my wife;
My father's murdered.

THE NAMELESS ONE

They died for the masses.
Erect barricades!
We're the defenders!
Our blood is ripe for battle!
Let them come!

[WORKMEN *storm into the hall.*]

FIFTH WORKMAN

They're butchering everyone.
Men, women, children.
We won't surrender to be killed
Like captured cattle!
They're butchering everyone; we must resist them to the end.
International law protects the enemy's soldiers,
But they can murder us like jungle beasts,
And set a premium on our flesh. . . .
Weapons are in our hands.
We're bringing bourgeoisie that we've captured;

I gave an order to shoot half of them.
We'll shoot the other half if their shock-troops get us.

THE NAMELESS ONE

You avenge your brothers.
Mass is revenge for the wrongs of centuries.
Mass is revenge.

THE WORKMEN

Is revenge!

THE WOMAN

Madmen, drunk with battle!
I stay your arms!
Mass should be a band of loving brothers.
Mass should be one firm community.
Community is not revenge.
Community tears up the roots of all injustice.
Community plants the flowers of righteousness.
The man who revenges himself creates nothing;
He only destroys.—
You shot half of your prisoners!
That was not self-defense?
Blind rage, not service to the cause.
You kill men.
Do you kill, with them, the spirit of the State
Which you are fighting? . . .
I'm going to help those men out there.

I was prepared
To cripple my own conscience
For the sake of the Mass.
I cry:
Break up the system!
But you—you want to break up men.
I can't keep silence, not to-day.
Out there are men,
Born in the blood of suffering mothers . . .
Men for ever brothers. . . .

THE NAMELESS ONE

For the last time, keep quiet, comrade.
Force . . . we need force. . . .
The enemy thinks nothing of our lives,
They will not spare us.
War is a grim affair; it can't be won
With pious looks.
Don't listen to this woman.
Prattle of petticoats!

THE WOMAN

I cry, Stop!
And you . . . who . . . are . . . you?
Are you driven by an unchained lust for power—
A lust that has been caged for centuries?
Who . . . are . . . you?

Murderer . . . or . . . Messiah . . . ?
Murderer . . . or . . . Messiah . . . ?
Nameless one—your face?
You are . . . ?

THE NAMELESS ONE

Mass!

THE WOMAN

You! . . . Mass!
I cannot bear you!
I must protect those men out there.
For many years I've walked along with you.
I know—you've suffered more than I. . . .
I have grown up in light and happy rooms,
Never knew hunger,
Never heard crazy laughter
Reeling from filthy hangings.
Still—I could feel for you
And know you.
See, I come to you now, a pleading child,
Quietly, humbly.
Listen to me:
Break down the pillars of injustice.
Break the old chains of hidden slavery.
But also break the weapons of a rotting age.
Shatter hate! Shatter revenge!
Revenge is not the purpose to reorganize.

Revenge is not Revolution.
Revenge is nothing but an axe that splits
The clean and glowing metal,
The power of Revolution.

THE NAMELESS ONE

How dare you, woman from another class,
Poison us in the hour of our decision?
I hear another accent in your talk.
You hope to shield those with whom you have grown up.
That's your real purpose.
You are betrayal.

CROWD IN THE HALL (*pressing threateningly about the* WOMAN)

Betrayal!

A CRY

An intellectual!

A CRY

To the wall with her!

THE NAMELESS ONE

Your shielding them is treason.
The hour calls for conflict,
Pitiless conflict.
Who is not with us is against us.
The Mass must triumph.

CROWD IN THE HALL

Must triumph!

THE NAMELESS ONE

You are arrested.

THE WOMAN

I . . . shield those . . . with whom I have grown up?
No—I shield you!
It is you who are standing there against the wall!
I shield your souls!
I shield humanity, divine humanity.
Insane accusers . . .
Is there fear in my words? . . .
Never as low as that . . .
I have chosen . . .
You lie . . . you lie . . .

[*A* WORKMAN *enters the hall.*]

WORKMAN

One of our prisoners barks,
Barks the same tune, barks all the time.
Wants to be taken to the woman who leads us.

THE NAMELESS ONE

Proof.

THE WOMAN

Again . . . you lie . . .
Who wants to speak to me—who?
Perhaps the man.
I never would betray my word for him.
But you betray yourselves . . .
I know nothing more. . . .

[*The* NAMELESS ONE *leaves the platform, diving into the crowd below him in the hall.* WORKERS *throng in from outside.*]

WORKERS

Lost!

CRIES

Fly! Slaughter!

[*Scattered shots outside. The* WORKERS *crowd to the door.*]

The door is blocked . . .
Caught like rats in a trap!

[*Silent waiting for death.*]

A CRY

We die!

[*Someone begins to sing the "Internationale." Others join in. Powerfully:*]

Awake, ye slaves of every nation,

Enchained to hunger, want, and shame.
The depths are loud with liberation;
The dawn grows bright—the torches flame.
The way is clear, old bonds are breaking;
Rise up, ye masses, seize command!
A new world's ours for the taking,
We slaves bring power where we stand.

Comrades of every nation,
March on, our flag's unfurled.
Arise to your salvation!
Arm, arm—and free the world!

[*Suddenly a short rattle of machine guns. The song is snapped off. The door at the principal entrance and the side doors are burst in with a single blow.* SOLDIERS *with guns in firing position stand at every door.*]

OFFICER

No use to resist!
Hands up!
Hands up, I command!
Where is the woman that leads you?
Why don't you stick up your hands?
Here—put on the handcuffs.
[SOLDIERS *handcuff the* WOMAN. *The stage darkens.*]

SIXTH PICTURE

Setting by Lee Simonson *Photograph by Francis Bruguiere*

Scene VI from The Theatre Guild Production

SIXTH PICTURE

(DREAM-PICTURE)

[*Boundless space. In the heart of it, a cage surrounded by a cone of light. Crouching within the cage is a handcuffed person who has the face of the* WOMAN. *Close to the cage is the* COMPANION *in the form of a* KEEPER.]

THE HANDCUFFED ONE

Where am
I?

THE KEEPER

In the place
Where man reviews himself.

THE HANDCUFFED ONE

Drive away the shadows.

THE KEEPER

Drive them away yourself.

[*A gray* SHADOW *without a head appears from somewhere.*]

FIRST SHADOW

You know me, one they shot to death?
Murderess!

THE HANDCUFFED ONE

I am not
Guilty.
[*A second gray* SHADOW *without a head appears from somewhere.*]

SECOND SHADOW

You murdered me,
Also.

THE HANDCUFFED ONE

You lie!
[*Other gray* SHADOWS *without heads emerge from somewhere.*]

THIRD SHADOW

You murdered me.

FOURTH SHADOW

And me.

FIFTH SHADOW

And me.

SIXTH SHADOW

And me.

THE HANDCUFFED ONE

Help me, keeper!
Good keeper!

THE KEEPER

Ha ha! Hahaha!

THE HANDCUFFED ONE

I did not want
Bloodshed.

FIRST SHADOW

You kept silent.

SECOND SHADOW

Silent when they attacked
The city hall.

THIRD SHADOW

Silent when they stole
The weapons.

FOURTH SHADOW

Silent when they fought.

FIFTH SHADOW

Silent when they went
For the reserves.

SIXTH SHADOW

You are guilty.

ALL THE SHADOWS

You are guilty.

THE HANDCUFFED ONE

I wanted
To save
The others
From shooting.

FIRST SHADOW

Don't deceive yourself.
Before that,
They shot us.

ALL THE SHADOWS

You murdered
All of us.

THE HANDCUFFED ONE

Then I am . . .

THE SHADOWS

Guilty!
Thrice guilty!

THE HANDCUFFED ONE

I . . . am . . . . guilty . . .
[*The* SHADOWS *fade.* BANKERS *in high silk hats emerge from somewhere.*]

FIRST BANKER

I offer
Guilty Bonds
At par

SECOND BANKER

Guilty Bonds
Are not listed
Any more.

THIRD BANKER

Bad investment!
Guilty Bonds,
Worthless scraps of paper.

THE THREE BANKERS

Guilty Bonds
Are a total loss.

[*The* HANDCUFFED ONE *raises herself up.*]

THE HANDCUFFED ONE

I . . . am . . . guilty.

[*The* BANKERS *fade.*]

THE KEEPER

Foolish one,
With your sentimental
Attitude to life—
If they were alive,
They would be dancing
About the golden altar
Where thousands have sacrificed.
And you, also.

THE HANDCUFFED ONE

I, Man, am guilty.

THE KEEPER

Mass is to blame.

THE HANDCUFFED ONE

Then I am doubly guilty.

THE KEEPER

Life is to blame.

THE HANDCUFFED ONE

And therefore must I
Assume the burden of its guilt?

THE KEEPER

Everyone lives in himself.
Everyone dies his own death.
Man,
Like every tree and flower,
Bound by destiny,
Moulded by patterns;
Ripening each in separate ways,
Withering by themselves . . .
Discover the answer for yourself!
Life is everything.

[*From somewhere,* PRISONERS *in their convicts' clothes enter, walking five paces apart. They have pointed caps on their heads, from which hang tattered rags concealing their faces and allowing room only for eye-holes. They walk, in a monotonous rhythm, silently around the cage.*]

THE HANDCUFFED ONE

Who are you,
Forms without faces?
Figures!
Who are you?

Mass
Of featureless forms?

DULL ECHO FROM A DISTANCE

Mass . . .

THE HANDCUFFED ONE

O God!

THE ECHO (*dying*)

Mass . . .

[*Silence drips.*]

THE HANDCUFFED ONE (*crying out*)

Mass is necessity!
Mass cannot be guilty!

THE KEEPER

Man cannot be guilty.

THE HANDCUFFED ONE

God is guilty!

DISTANT ECHOES

Guilty . . .
Guilty . . .
Guilty . . .

THE KEEPER

God is within you.

THE HANDCUFFED ONE

Then I will triumph over God.

THE KEEPER

Worm!
Blasphemer!

THE HANDCUFFED ONE

Did I dishonour
God?
Or did God
Dishonour Man?
O frightful
Decrees of guilt,
In which
Man after man
Is horribly entangled.
God—
Bring God to justice!
I accuse him!

ECHO FROM A DISTANCE

Bring God to justice!
[*The moving* PRISONERS *stand still. Their arms suddenly shoot up.*]

THE PRISONERS

We accuse Him!

[*The* PRISONERS *fade.*]

THE KEEPER

Now you are healed.
Come out
Of the cage.

THE HANDCUFFED ONE

I am free?

THE KEEPER

Fettered!
Free!

[*The stage darkens.*]

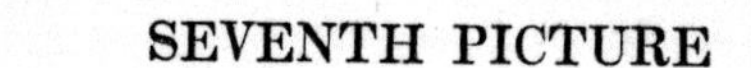

SEVENTH PICTURE

Setting by Lee Simonson *Photograph by Francis Bruguiere*

Scene VII from The Theatre Guild Production

SEVENTH PICTURE

[*A prison cell. A small table, bench, and iron bed fastened to the wall. A grated hole of light clouded by frosted glass. The* WOMAN *sits at the table.*]

THE WOMAN

O path that leads through fields of ripening wheat
In August days . . .
Wandering on wintry hills before the dawn . . .
O beetle drinking in the breath of noon . . .
O world . . .

[*Silence spreads itself gently about the* WOMAN.]

Did I long for a child?

[*Silence soars.*]

How life divides us all in two!
Bound to man and his desires.
To those we love . . . and hate . . .
Bound to our enemies?
Bound to ourselves?
I need him now . . . he must confirm me.

[*The cell is unlocked. The* MAN *enters.*]

THE MAN

Wife . . . I have come,
Come because you called me.

THE WOMAN

Husband . . . !
Man . . .

THE MAN

I bring good news.
The sewers cannot keep on pouring
Their filth upon your name . . . my name, whenever they like.
The investigation of the recent murders
Showed that you were not guilty of the outrageous shootings.
Courage! The sentence committing you to death
Has not yet been confirmed.
In spite of treason to the State,
The nobility of aim
Is always respected
By all right-thinking people.

THE WOMAN (*crying softly*)

I am without guilt . . .
Without guilt . . . yet I am guilty . . .

THE MAN

You are not guilty.
That's positive to every right-thinking person.

THE WOMAN

To every right-thinking person . . .
I am so hurt . . .
And glad, because your name, free of disgrace . . .

THE MAN

I knew you were not guilty.

THE WOMAN

Yes . . . you knew it . . .
Respect for good intentions . . .
You're so respectable!
I see you now so clearly . . .
And yet it's you who have been guilty—husband,
You . . . guilty of all these deaths.

THE MAN

Wife, I came to you . . .
Wife . . . your speech is hate.

THE WOMAN

Hate? Never hate.
I love you—love you with all my blood.

THE MAN

I warned you against the masses.
Root up the masses and you root up hell.

THE WOMAN

Hell? Who made that hell?
Who built the torture of your golden mills
That grind and grind out profit day by day?
Who put up prisons . . . who cried "holy war"?
Who sacrificed a million human lives
Upon the altars of some desperate game?
Who threw the masses into festering holes
In which, each day, is piled the filth of yesterday?
Who robbed these brothers of their human features,
Who drove them into factories,
Debased them into parts of a machine?
The State! . . . You! . . .

THE MAN

My life is duty.

THE WOMAN

Oh, yes . . . duty . . . duty to the State.
You're so respectable . . .
Didn't I say I saw you all too clearly?
You've been so well brought up.
You—tell all your right-thinking people

They never have been right . . .
They are the guilty ones . . .
We are all guilty . . .
Yes, I am guilty . . . guilty to myself,
Guilty to all mankind.

THE MAN

I came to you.
Is this a court of justice?

THE WOMAN

Here is a court of justice!
I, the accused, am also judge.
I bring the accusation . . . and pass sentence;
Pronounce acquittal
And the final blame . . .
Can you surmise . . . who bears the final blame?
Men must desire to work,
And work grows red with the dear blood of men.
Men must desire to live,
And they must swim through seas of human blood.
Can you surmise . . . who bears the final blame? . . .
Come, give me your hand,
Beloved of my blood.
I have conquered myself . . .
Myself and you.

[*The* MAN *breaks into trembling. A thought, suddenly springing up, distorts his face. He stumbles out.*]

THE WOMAN

Give me your hand . . .
Brother, give me your hand;
You also are my brother.—
You have gone . . . you had to go . . .
The last road runs across a snowfield.
The last road never knows companions.
The last road winds without a mother.
The last road we walk alone.
[*The door is opened. The* NAMELESS ONE *enters.*]

THE NAMELESS ONE

Cured of illusions? Free of dusty dreams?
Has knowledge thrust a dagger through your heart?
Did the judge say "human" and "you are forgiven"?
It was a wholesome lesson.
I congratulate you on your conversion.
Now you are ours again.

THE WOMAN

You! Who sent you?

THE NAMELESS ONE

The masses.

THE WOMAN

They've not forgotten me?
The message . . . the message . . .

THE NAMELESS ONE

My mission here is to set you free.

THE WOMAN

Freedom!
Life!
We escape? Is everything prepared?

THE NAMELESS ONE

Two keepers have been bribed.
There's one more at the gate. I'll strike him down.

THE WOMAN

You'd murder him . . . for me?

THE NAMELESS ONE

For the cause.

THE WOMAN

I have no right
To win life through a keeper's death.

THE NAMELESS ONE

The masses have a right to you.

THE WOMAN

And the rights of the keeper?
Keepers are men.

THE NAMELESS ONE

We have no "men" as yet.
On one side, the group belonging to the mass.
On the other, the class belonging to the State.

THE WOMAN

Man is naked.

THE NAMELESS ONE

Mass is godlike.

THE WOMAN

Mass is not godlike.
Force made the mass.
Evils of property made the mass.
Mass is the movement of distress,
Is meek devotion . . .
Is terrible vengeance . . .
Is blinded slavery . . .
Is holy purpose . . .

Mass is a fertile field that has been trampled;
Mass is the choked-up, inarticulate people.

THE NAMELESS ONE

And action?

THE WOMAN

Action! And more than action!
To free man in the mass;
To free community in the mass.

THE NAMELESS ONE

The raw wind before the gates
Will heal you.
Hurry!
We have only a few minutes left.

THE WOMAN

You are not deliverance.
You are not salvation.
But I know who you are.
"Kill him!" you cried. Always your cry is "Kill him!"
Your father's name is War.
You are his bastard.
You poor, new head-of-staff of executioners,
Your only remedy: "Death!" and "Shoot them down!"

Throw off the mantle of your lofty phrases,
There's nothing but a woven tissue of lies.

THE NAMELESS ONE

The murder-generals battled for the State!

THE WOMAN

They murdered, but they did not kill with joy.
Like you, they all believed in their own mission.

THE NAMELESS ONE

They battled for the cold, tyrannical State;
We battle for humanity!

THE WOMAN

You murder for humanity,
As those deluded ones murdered for the State.
And there were some who surely felt
That through their State, their fatherland,
The earth would be redeemed.
I see no difference:
These murder for a single country,
The others kill for every country.
These murder for a thousand people,
The others for a million.
The one who murders for the State,
You call an executioner.

But he who murders for mankind
Is called a saviour; you crown him
Courageous, noble, great.
Yes, you can speak of good and holy violence!

THE NAMELESS ONE

Rail against others, rail against life itself!
Should I let still more millions be enslaved
Because their enslavers chain them in good faith?
And are you the less guilty
If you keep silent?

THE WOMAN

The torch of gloomy violence cannot show the way.
You lead us to a new and curious land,
The land of ancient human slavery.
If fate has pushed you forward at this time
And given you a reckless power
To blandish and betray the desperate crowds
Who look to you as to a new Messiah,
I know this—such a fate will turn against the man.

THE NAMELESS ONE

Mass counts and not the man.
You're not our heroine, our one-time leader.
Each person bears the taint of their extraction;
You have the bourgeois symptoms:
Weakness and self-deception.

THE WOMAN

You have no love for man.

THE NAMELESS ONE

The principle above everything!
I love posterity!

THE WOMAN

The individual above everything!
You—you would sacrifice
All living men
For a principle.

THE NAMELESS ONE

The principle demands the sacrifice.
But you betray the masses; you betray the cause.
These are the days when one must make decisions.
Who hesitates and lacks determination,
Supports the masters who bear down upon us,
Supports the masters who have let us hunger,
Is our foe.

THE WOMAN

I would betray the masses
If I demanded a single human life.
A leader has no right to sacrifice any one but himself.
Listen: no man has the right to kill another

To forward any cause,
And any cause demanding it is damned!
Whoever, in its name, calls for the blood of man
Is Moloch.
God was Moloch.
State was Moloch.
Mass was Moloch.

THE NAMELESS ONE

And what is holy?

THE WOMAN

Some day . . .
Brotherhood . . .
Free men bound only by their common work . . .
Work . . . People.

THE NAMELESS ONE

You lack the power to face the unyielding fact,
The need to act.
Free men will only come
Through hard facts and through harder deeds!
Atone by dying.
Perhaps your death will be some use to us.

THE WOMAN

I live for ever.

THE NAMELESS ONE

You were born too soon.

[*The* NAMELESS ONE *leaves the cell.*]

THE WOMAN

You lived yesterday.
You live to-day.
And you are dead to-morrow.
I live for ever,
From sphere to sphere,
From change to change,
Till some day I become
Clean,
Guiltless,
Mankind.

[*A* PRIEST *enters.*]

THE PRIEST

I come to give you final consolation;
The Church does not refuse assistance even to the criminal.

THE WOMAN

By whose orders?

THE PRIEST

The State authorities directed me.

THE WOMAN

Where were you on the day of the trial?
Leave me!

THE PRIEST

God forgives you, too. I understand you.
You thought mankind was good—or so you dreamed—
And you allowed outrage and sacrilege
Against the holy State and sacred order.
Man is all evil—bad from the beginning.

THE WOMAN

Man longs for goodness.

THE PRIEST

The lie of these degenerate days,
Born of despair, decay, and effort to escape,
Protected by a brittle shell
Of pitiful and empty faith,
Forced by a bad conscience.
Believe me, he never once desires to be good.

THE WOMAN

He longs for goodness. Even when he does wrong,
He does it under the mask of doing good.

THE PRIEST

Nations come, nations go;
This earth has never seen paradise.

THE WOMAN

I believe.

THE PRIEST

Remember:
Lust for power; lust for pleasure!
That is the rhythm of the world.

THE WOMAN

I believe!

THE PRIEST

Earthly life is a constant changing of forms.
Mankind stays helpless. Salvation rests in God.

THE WOMAN

I believe!!!
I am cold . . . Leave me!
Leave me!

[*The* PRIEST *leaves the cell. An* OFFICER *enters.*]

THE OFFICER

Here's the sentence.
Mitigating circumstances considered.
Nevertheless. Crimes against State must be punished.

THE WOMAN

They are going to shoot me?

THE OFFICER

Orders are orders. Obedience, obedience.
State interests; quiet, discipline.
Duty as officer.

THE WOMAN

And man?

THE OFFICER

All conversation forbidden.
Orders are orders.

THE WOMAN

I am ready.

[*The* OFFICER *and the* WOMAN *go out. The cell is empty for a few seconds. Two* WOMAN PRISONERS *in prison smocks slip in. They remain standing at the door.*]

FIRST PRISONER

Did you see the officer? See his lovely gold uniform?

SECOND PRISONER

I saw the coffin. In the laundry. Yellow wooden box.

[*The* FIRST PRISONER *sees bread lying on the table and throws herself upon it.*]

FIRST PRISONER

There's bread! Hungry! Hungry! Hungry!

SECOND PRISONER

Give me! Me bread! Me bread!

FIRST PRISONER

Here's a mirror. My, how pretty!
Hide it. Evening. Cell.

SECOND PRISONER

Here's a silky cloth.
Naked breast, silky cloth.
Hide it. Evening. Cell.

[*From outside the sharp crack of a volley rings through the cell. The* PRISONERS *throw up outstretched, frightened hands. The* FIRST PRISONER *searches in her skirt for the mirror she has hidden. Lays it hurriedly back on the table and cries, sinking upon her knees.*]

FIRST PRISONER

Sister, why did we do that?

[*Her arms toss in the air with a great helplessness. The* SECOND PRISONER *takes the silken cloth which she has hidden in her skirt and lays it hurriedly on the bed.*]

SECOND PRISONER

Sister, why did we do that?

[*The* SECOND PRISONER *breaks down. She buries her head in her lap. The curtain falls.*]